THIS DELUXE HOME
MAINTENANCE LOGBOOK
BELONGS TO:

_____

address: _____

_____

ABOUT THIS HOUSE:

square feet:	style:	
year built:	lot #:	
# of rooms:	# bedrooms:	# baths:
move in date:	# of previous owners:	

Deluxe
HOME MAINTENANCE
LOG BOOK

TABLE OF *Contents*

	PAGE
Important Contacts (local & professional)	4
Where Is It?	6
Maintenance/Service Log (appliances, systems, etc.)	8
Home Maintenance Check List Suggestions	12
12 Years of Seasonal/Monthly Home Maintenance	14
Safety Inspections Log (alarms, fire extinguishers, etc.)	86
12 Years of Home Security System Inspections	88
HVAC Filters Log	92
Pest Control Log	94
Home Improvement Wishlist	96
Home Upgrade Log	100
Painting Log	104
Room by Room Logs (document upgrades)	108
Room Inventory (for insurance purposes)	152
DIY Project Log (track budget, action steps, & materials needed)	166

IMPORTANT *Contacts*

NAME	PHONE	LOCAL COMPANY NAME	WEBSITE
Police		
Fire		
Trash Removal		
Recycling		
Phone/Cable/Satellite		
Homeowners Association		
Village/Township Admin		
Voting Precinct		

NOTES

IMPORTANT *Contacts*

PROFESSIONAL

NAME	PHONE	COMPANY NAME ⋮ WEBSITE
Electrician		
Plumber		
HAVC		
Roofer		
Handyman		
Lawncare		
Sprinkler System		
Pool		
Hardscapes		
Windows/Siding		
Homeowners Insurance		
Home Security System		

NOTES

Where IS IT?

Water Heater	HVAC Units	Electrical Box	Water Meter & Main Shut-Off

Gas Meter & Main Shut-Off	Sprinkler Controls		

NOTES

Where IS IT?

Smoke Detectors

Carbon Monoxide Detectors

Fire Extinguisher(s)

Attic Entrance(s)

Sump Pump(s)

Thermostats

Home Security Panel

NOTES

MAINTENANCE/SERVICE *Log*

Keep track of home service calls & repairs

DATE	SYSTEM/APPLIANCE	PROBLEM

CONTACT PHONE #	HOW WAS IT RESOLVED	SATISFACTION RATING

MAINTENANCE/SERVICE *log*

Keep track of home service calls & repairs

DATE	SYSTEM/APPLIANCE	PROBLEM

CONTACT PHONE #	HOW WAS IT RESOLVED	SATISFACTION RATING

HOME MAINTENANCE CHECK LIST *Suggestions*

MONTHLY
- Inspect, and possibly change out HVAC filters.
- Clean the garbage disposal by grinding ice cubes, then flushing with hot water and baking soda.
- Clean range hood filters.
- Inspect your fire extinguisher(s).
- Inspect tub and sink drains for debris; unclog.
- Inspect electrical cords for wear.
- Vacuum heat registers and heat vents.

QUARTERLY
- Test smoke/carbon dioxide detectors.
- Test garage door auto-reverse feature.
- Run water and flush toilets in unused spaces.
- Check water softener, add salt if needed.
- Clean dryer vents.

BI-ANNUALLY
- Give your house a deep clean.
- Test your water heater's pressure relief valve.
- Vacuum your refrigerator coils.

SPRING
- Check the exterior drainage.
- Clean out gutters.
- Inspect the exterior of your home.
- Change the air-conditioner filter.
- Get your air conditioning system ready for summer; consider having it professionally serviced.
- Repair/replace damaged window screens.
- Check trees for interference with electric lines .
- Clear dead plants/shrubs from the house.
- Inspect roofing for damage, leaks, etc.
- Clean window and door screens.
- Refinish the deck.
- Replace the batteries in smoke and carbon monoxide detectors.
- Fertilize your lawn.
- Remove leaves and debris from gutters and downspouts.
- Get your lawnmower ready for use: spark plugs, clean & sharpen blades, drain fuel or add stabilizer, clean motor and it's parts.

SUMMER

- Check your sprinkler system or hire a professional.
- Check grout in bathrooms, kitchen, etc.; repair as needed.
- Take care of any insect problems. Call a professional if needed.
- Inspect plumbing for leaks, clean aerators on faucets.
- Clean and repair deck/patio as needed.
- Clean out window wells of debris.
- Check and clean dryer vent, other exhaust vents to exterior of home.
- Clean garage.
- Oil garage-door opener and chain, garage door, and all door hinges.
- Remove lint from inside and outside washer hoses and dryer vents.
- Clean kitchen exhaust fan filter.
- Check dishwasher for leaks.
- Check around kitchen and bathroom cabinets and around toilets for leaks.
- Replace interior and exterior faucet and showerhead washers if needed.
- Seal tile grout.
- Prune trees and shrubs.
- Good time to repair & paint the exterior as needed.
- Check attic, crawl spaces for critters. Call a pest specialist if needed.
- Replace caulking and weather stripping around doors and windows as needed.
- Check your fireplace and chimney or have it serviced by a professional.

FALL

- Flush hot water heater and remove sediment.
- Winterize air conditioning systems.
- Get heating system ready for winter.
- Turn off and flush outdoor water faucets.
- Get chimney cleaned.
- Test sump pump.
- Check driveway/pavement for cracks.
- Check your winter gear supply –ice melting products, snow shovels.
- Clean & prepare snowblower.
- Rake leaves and aerate the lawn.
- Inspect roofing for missing, loose, or damaged shingles and leaks.
- Power-wash windows and siding.
- Replace the batteries in smoke and carbon monoxide detectors. Install a smoke detector on every floor of your home, including the basement.
- Drain and store hoses.
- Wrap insulation around outdoor faucets and pipes in unheated garages.
- Prepare sprinkler system for winter or call a professional to winterize them.

WINTER

- Regularly check for ice dams and icicles.
- Tighten any handles, knobs, racks, etc.
- Check all locks and deadbolts on your doors and windows.
- Check caulking around showers and bathtubs; repair as needed.
- Remove showerheads and clean sediment.
- Deep clean and inspect the basement.
- Cover your air-conditioning unit.
- Check basement for leaks during thaws.
- Vacuum bathroom exhaust fan grill.

SPRING MAINTENANCE

INDOOR

- ○ _____
- ○ _____
- ○ _____
- ○ _____
- ○ _____
- ○ _____
- ○ _____

OUTDOOR

- ○ _____
- ○ _____
- ○ _____
- ○ _____
- ○ _____
- ○ _____
- ○ _____

NOTES

SUMMER MAINTENANCE

INDOOR

- ○ _____
- ○ _____
- ○ _____
- ○ _____
- ○ _____
- ○ _____
- ○ _____

OUTDOOR

- ○ _____
- ○ _____
- ○ _____
- ○ _____
- ○ _____
- ○ _____
- ○ _____

NOTES

YEAR

FALL MAINTENANCE

INDOOR

- ◯ _____
- ◯ _____
- ◯ _____
- ◯ _____
- ◯ _____
- ◯ _____
- ◯ _____

OUTDOOR

- ◯ _____
- ◯ _____
- ◯ _____
- ◯ _____
- ◯ _____
- ◯ _____
- ◯ _____

NOTES

WINTER MAINTENANCE

INDOOR

- ◯ _____
- ◯ _____
- ◯ _____
- ◯ _____
- ◯ _____
- ◯ _____
- ◯ _____

OUTDOOR

- ◯ _____
- ◯ _____
- ◯ _____
- ◯ _____
- ◯ _____
- ◯ _____
- ◯ _____

NOTES

Indoor **MONTHLY MAINTENANCE**

JANUARY

- ◯ _____
- ◯ _____
- ◯ _____
- ◯ _____
- ◯ _____
- ◯ _____
- ◯ _____

FEBRUARY

- ◯ _____
- ◯ _____
- ◯ _____
- ◯ _____
- ◯ _____
- ◯ _____
- ◯ _____

MARCH

- ◯ _____
- ◯ _____
- ◯ _____
- ◯ _____
- ◯ _____
- ◯ _____
- ◯ _____

APRIL

- ◯ _____
- ◯ _____
- ◯ _____
- ◯ _____
- ◯ _____
- ◯ _____
- ◯ _____

MAY

- ◯ _____
- ◯ _____
- ◯ _____
- ◯ _____
- ◯ _____
- ◯ _____
- ◯ _____

JUNE

- ◯ _____
- ◯ _____
- ◯ _____
- ◯ _____
- ◯ _____
- ◯ _____
- ◯ _____

JULY

- ◯ _____
- ◯ _____
- ◯ _____
- ◯ _____
- ◯ _____
- ◯ _____
- ◯ _____

AUGUST

- ◯ _____
- ◯ _____
- ◯ _____
- ◯ _____
- ◯ _____
- ◯ _____
- ◯ _____

SEPTEMBER

- ◯ _____
- ◯ _____
- ◯ _____
- ◯ _____
- ◯ _____
- ◯ _____
- ◯ _____

OCTOBER

- ◯ _____
- ◯ _____
- ◯ _____
- ◯ _____
- ◯ _____
- ◯ _____
- ◯ _____

NOVEMBER

- ◯ _____
- ◯ _____
- ◯ _____
- ◯ _____
- ◯ _____
- ◯ _____
- ◯ _____

DECEMBER

- ◯ _____
- ◯ _____
- ◯ _____
- ◯ _____
- ◯ _____
- ◯ _____
- ◯ _____

Outdoor MONTHLY MAINTENANCE

JANUARY

- ◯ _____
- ◯ _____
- ◯ _____
- ◯ _____
- ◯ _____
- ◯ _____
- ◯ _____

FEBRUARY

- ◯ _____
- ◯ _____
- ◯ _____
- ◯ _____
- ◯ _____
- ◯ _____
- ◯ _____

MARCH

- ◯ _____
- ◯ _____
- ◯ _____
- ◯ _____
- ◯ _____
- ◯ _____
- ◯ _____

APRIL

- ◯ _____
- ◯ _____
- ◯ _____
- ◯ _____
- ◯ _____
- ◯ _____
- ◯ _____

MAY

- ◯ _____
- ◯ _____
- ◯ _____
- ◯ _____
- ◯ _____
- ◯ _____
- ◯ _____

JUNE

- ◯ _____
- ◯ _____
- ◯ _____
- ◯ _____
- ◯ _____
- ◯ _____
- ◯ _____

JULY

- ◯ _____
- ◯ _____
- ◯ _____
- ◯ _____
- ◯ _____
- ◯ _____
- ◯ _____

AUGUST

- ◯ _____
- ◯ _____
- ◯ _____
- ◯ _____
- ◯ _____
- ◯ _____
- ◯ _____

SEPTEMBER

- ◯ _____
- ◯ _____
- ◯ _____
- ◯ _____
- ◯ _____
- ◯ _____
- ◯ _____

OCTOBER

- ◯ _____
- ◯ _____
- ◯ _____
- ◯ _____
- ◯ _____
- ◯ _____
- ◯ _____

NOVEMBER

- ◯ _____
- ◯ _____
- ◯ _____
- ◯ _____
- ◯ _____
- ◯ _____

DECEMBER

- ◯ _____
- ◯ _____
- ◯ _____
- ◯ _____
- ◯ _____
- ◯ _____
- ◯ _____

WHAT TO DO DIFFERENT NEXT YEAR:

SPRING MAINTENANCE

INDOOR

- ○ _____
- ○ _____
- ○ _____
- ○ _____
- ○ _____
- ○ _____
- ○ _____

OUTDOOR

- ○ _____
- ○ _____
- ○ _____
- ○ _____
- ○ _____
- ○ _____
- ○ _____

NOTES

SUMMER MAINTENANCE

INDOOR

- ○ _____
- ○ _____
- ○ _____
- ○ _____
- ○ _____
- ○ _____
- ○ _____

OUTDOOR

- ○ _____
- ○ _____
- ○ _____
- ○ _____
- ○ _____
- ○ _____
- ○ _____

NOTES

FALL MAINTENANCE

INDOOR

- ◯ _____
- ◯ _____
- ◯ _____
- ◯ _____
- ◯ _____
- ◯ _____
- ◯ _____

OUTDOOR

- ◯ _____
- ◯ _____
- ◯ _____
- ◯ _____
- ◯ _____
- ◯ _____
- ◯ _____

NOTES

WINTER MAINTENANCE

INDOOR

- ◯ _____
- ◯ _____
- ◯ _____
- ◯ _____
- ◯ _____
- ◯ _____
- ◯ _____

OUTDOOR

- ◯ _____
- ◯ _____
- ◯ _____
- ◯ _____
- ◯ _____
- ◯ _____
- ◯ _____

NOTES

Indoor MONTHLY MAINTENANCE

JANUARY
- ◯ _____
- ◯ _____
- ◯ _____
- ◯ _____
- ◯ _____
- ◯ _____
- ◯ _____

FEBRUARY
- ◯ _____
- ◯ _____
- ◯ _____
- ◯ _____
- ◯ _____
- ◯ _____
- ◯ _____

MARCH
- ◯ _____
- ◯ _____
- ◯ _____
- ◯ _____
- ◯ _____
- ◯ _____
- ◯ _____

APRIL
- ◯ _____
- ◯ _____
- ◯ _____
- ◯ _____
- ◯ _____
- ◯ _____
- ◯ _____

MAY
- ◯ _____
- ◯ _____
- ◯ _____
- ◯ _____
- ◯ _____
- ◯ _____
- ◯ _____

JUNE
- ◯ _____
- ◯ _____
- ◯ _____
- ◯ _____
- ◯ _____
- ◯ _____
- ◯ _____

JULY
- ◯ _____
- ◯ _____
- ◯ _____
- ◯ _____
- ◯ _____
- ◯ _____
- ◯ _____

AUGUST
- ◯ _____
- ◯ _____
- ◯ _____
- ◯ _____
- ◯ _____
- ◯ _____
- ◯ _____

SEPTEMBER
- ◯ _____
- ◯ _____
- ◯ _____
- ◯ _____
- ◯ _____
- ◯ _____
- ◯ _____

OCTOBER
- ◯ _____
- ◯ _____
- ◯ _____
- ◯ _____
- ◯ _____
- ◯ _____
- ◯ _____

NOVEMBER
- ◯ _____
- ◯ _____
- ◯ _____
- ◯ _____
- ◯ _____
- ◯ _____
- ◯ _____

DECEMBER
- ◯ _____
- ◯ _____
- ◯ _____
- ◯ _____
- ◯ _____
- ◯ _____
- ◯ _____

Outdoor MONTHLY MAINTENANCE

JANUARY

- ◯
- ◯
- ◯
- ◯
- ◯
- ◯
- ◯

FEBRUARY

- ◯
- ◯
- ◯
- ◯
- ◯
- ◯
- ◯

MARCH

- ◯
- ◯
- ◯
- ◯
- ◯
- ◯
- ◯

APRIL

- ◯
- ◯
- ◯
- ◯
- ◯
- ◯
- ◯

MAY

- ◯
- ◯
- ◯
- ◯
- ◯
- ◯
- ◯

JUNE

- ◯
- ◯
- ◯
- ◯
- ◯
- ◯
- ◯

JULY

- ◯
- ◯
- ◯
- ◯
- ◯
- ◯
- ◯

AUGUST

- ◯
- ◯
- ◯
- ◯
- ◯
- ◯
- ◯

SEPTEMBER

- ◯
- ◯
- ◯
- ◯
- ◯
- ◯
- ◯

OCTOBER

- ◯
- ◯
- ◯
- ◯
- ◯
- ◯
- ◯

NOVEMBER

- ◯
- ◯
- ◯
- ◯
- ◯
- ◯

DECEMBER

- ◯
- ◯
- ◯
- ◯
- ◯
- ◯

WHAT TO DO DIFFERENT NEXT YEAR:

SPRING MAINTENANCE

INDOOR

- ○ _____
- ○ _____
- ○ _____
- ○ _____
- ○ _____
- ○ _____
- ○ _____

OUTDOOR

- ○ _____
- ○ _____
- ○ _____
- ○ _____
- ○ _____
- ○ _____
- ○ _____

NOTES

SUMMER MAINTENANCE

INDOOR

- ○ _____
- ○ _____
- ○ _____
- ○ _____
- ○ _____
- ○ _____
- ○ _____

OUTDOOR

- ○ _____
- ○ _____
- ○ _____
- ○ _____
- ○ _____
- ○ _____
- ○ _____

NOTES

FALL MAINTENANCE

INDOOR

- ○ _____
- ○ _____
- ○ _____
- ○ _____
- ○ _____
- ○ _____
- ○ _____

OUTDOOR

- ○ _____
- ○ _____
- ○ _____
- ○ _____
- ○ _____
- ○ _____
- ○ _____

NOTES

WINTER MAINTENANCE

INDOOR

- ○ _____
- ○ _____
- ○ _____
- ○ _____
- ○ _____
- ○ _____
- ○ _____

OUTDOOR

- ○ _____
- ○ _____
- ○ _____
- ○ _____
- ○ _____
- ○ _____
- ○ _____

NOTES

Indoor MONTHLY MAINTENANCE

JANUARY

- ◯
- ◯
- ◯
- ◯
- ◯
- ◯
- ◯

FEBRUARY

- ◯
- ◯
- ◯
- ◯
- ◯
- ◯
- ◯

MARCH

- ◯
- ◯
- ◯
- ◯
- ◯
- ◯
- ◯

APRIL

- ◯
- ◯
- ◯
- ◯
- ◯
- ◯
- ◯

MAY

- ◯
- ◯
- ◯
- ◯
- ◯
- ◯
- ◯

JUNE

- ◯
- ◯
- ◯
- ◯
- ◯
- ◯
- ◯

JULY

- ◯
- ◯
- ◯
- ◯
- ◯
- ◯
- ◯

AUGUST

- ◯
- ◯
- ◯
- ◯
- ◯
- ◯
- ◯

SEPTEMBER

- ◯
- ◯
- ◯
- ◯
- ◯
- ◯
- ◯

OCTOBER

- ◯
- ◯
- ◯
- ◯
- ◯
- ◯
- ◯

NOVEMBER

- ◯
- ◯
- ◯
- ◯
- ◯
- ◯

DECEMBER

- ◯
- ◯
- ◯
- ◯
- ◯
- ◯
- ◯

Outdoor MONTHLY MAINTENANCE

JANUARY

- ○
- ○
- ○
- ○
- ○
- ○
- ○

FEBRUARY

- ○
- ○
- ○
- ○
- ○
- ○
- ○

MARCH

- ○
- ○
- ○
- ○
- ○
- ○
- ○

APRIL

- ○
- ○
- ○
- ○
- ○
- ○
- ○

MAY

- ○
- ○
- ○
- ○
- ○
- ○
- ○

JUNE

- ○
- ○
- ○
- ○
- ○
- ○
- ○

JULY

- ○
- ○
- ○
- ○
- ○
- ○
- ○

AUGUST

- ○
- ○
- ○
- ○
- ○
- ○
- ○

SEPTEMBER

- ○
- ○
- ○
- ○
- ○
- ○
- ○

OCTOBER

- ○
- ○
- ○
- ○
- ○
- ○
- ○

NOVEMBER

- ○
- ○
- ○
- ○
- ○
- ○
- ○

DECEMBER

- ○
- ○
- ○
- ○
- ○
- ○
- ○

WHAT TO DO DIFFERENT NEXT YEAR:

SPRING MAINTENANCE

INDOOR

- ○ _____
- ○ _____
- ○ _____
- ○ _____
- ○ _____
- ○ _____
- ○ _____

OUTDOOR

- ○ _____
- ○ _____
- ○ _____
- ○ _____
- ○ _____
- ○ _____
- ○ _____

NOTES

SUMMER MAINTENANCE

INDOOR

- ○ _____
- ○ _____
- ○ _____
- ○ _____
- ○ _____
- ○ _____
- ○ _____

OUTDOOR

- ○ _____
- ○ _____
- ○ _____
- ○ _____
- ○ _____
- ○ _____
- ○ _____

NOTES

FALL MAINTENANCE

INDOOR

- ○ ....
- ○ ....
- ○ ....
- ○ ....
- ○ ....
- ○ ....
- ○ ....

OUTDOOR

- ○ ....
- ○ ....
- ○ ....
- ○ ....
- ○ ....
- ○ ....
- ○ ....

NOTES

WINTER MAINTENANCE

INDOOR

- ○ ....
- ○ ....
- ○ ....
- ○ ....
- ○ ....
- ○ ....
- ○ ....

OUTDOOR

- ○ ....
- ○ ....
- ○ ....
- ○ ....
- ○ ....
- ○ ....
- ○ ....

NOTES

Indoor MONTHLY MAINTENANCE

JANUARY

- ◯ _____
- ◯ _____
- ◯ _____
- ◯ _____
- ◯ _____
- ◯ _____
- ◯ _____

FEBRUARY

- ◯ _____
- ◯ _____
- ◯ _____
- ◯ _____
- ◯ _____
- ◯ _____
- ◯ _____

MARCH

- ◯ _____
- ◯ _____
- ◯ _____
- ◯ _____
- ◯ _____
- ◯ _____
- ◯ _____

APRIL

- ◯ _____
- ◯ _____
- ◯ _____
- ◯ _____
- ◯ _____
- ◯ _____
- ◯ _____

MAY

- ◯ _____
- ◯ _____
- ◯ _____
- ◯ _____
- ◯ _____
- ◯ _____
- ◯ _____

JUNE

- ◯ _____
- ◯ _____
- ◯ _____
- ◯ _____
- ◯ _____
- ◯ _____
- ◯ _____

JULY

- ◯ _____
- ◯ _____
- ◯ _____
- ◯ _____
- ◯ _____
- ◯ _____
- ◯ _____

AUGUST

- ◯ _____
- ◯ _____
- ◯ _____
- ◯ _____
- ◯ _____
- ◯ _____
- ◯ _____

SEPTEMBER

- ◯ _____
- ◯ _____
- ◯ _____
- ◯ _____
- ◯ _____
- ◯ _____
- ◯ _____

OCTOBER

- ◯ _____
- ◯ _____
- ◯ _____
- ◯ _____
- ◯ _____
- ◯ _____
- ◯ _____

NOVEMBER

- ◯ _____
- ◯ _____
- ◯ _____
- ◯ _____
- ◯ _____
- ◯ _____

DECEMBER

- ◯ _____
- ◯ _____
- ◯ _____
- ◯ _____
- ◯ _____
- ◯ _____
- ◯ _____

Outdoor MONTHLY MAINTENANCE

JANUARY

- ◯ _____
- ◯ _____
- ◯ _____
- ◯ _____
- ◯ _____
- ◯ _____
- ◯ _____

FEBRUARY

- ◯ _____
- ◯ _____
- ◯ _____
- ◯ _____
- ◯ _____
- ◯ _____
- ◯ _____

MARCH

- ◯ _____
- ◯ _____
- ◯ _____
- ◯ _____
- ◯ _____
- ◯ _____
- ◯ _____

APRIL

- ◯ _____
- ◯ _____
- ◯ _____
- ◯ _____
- ◯ _____
- ◯ _____
- ◯ _____

MAY

- ◯ _____
- ◯ _____
- ◯ _____
- ◯ _____
- ◯ _____
- ◯ _____
- ◯ _____

JUNE

- ◯ _____
- ◯ _____
- ◯ _____
- ◯ _____
- ◯ _____
- ◯ _____
- ◯ _____

JULY

- ◯ _____
- ◯ _____
- ◯ _____
- ◯ _____
- ◯ _____
- ◯ _____
- ◯ _____

AUGUST

- ◯ _____
- ◯ _____
- ◯ _____
- ◯ _____
- ◯ _____
- ◯ _____
- ◯ _____

SEPTEMBER

- ◯ _____
- ◯ _____
- ◯ _____
- ◯ _____
- ◯ _____
- ◯ _____
- ◯ _____

OCTOBER

- ◯ _____
- ◯ _____
- ◯ _____
- ◯ _____
- ◯ _____
- ◯ _____
- ◯ _____

NOVEMBER

- ◯ _____
- ◯ _____
- ◯ _____
- ◯ _____
- ◯ _____
- ◯ _____

DECEMBER

- ◯ _____
- ◯ _____
- ◯ _____
- ◯ _____
- ◯ _____
- ◯ _____
- ◯ _____

WHAT TO DO DIFFERENT NEXT YEAR:

SPRING MAINTENANCE

INDOOR

- ○ _____
- ○ _____
- ○ _____
- ○ _____
- ○ _____
- ○ _____
- ○ _____

OUTDOOR

- ○ _____
- ○ _____
- ○ _____
- ○ _____
- ○ _____
- ○ _____
- ○ _____

NOTES

SUMMER MAINTENANCE

INDOOR

- ○ _____
- ○ _____
- ○ _____
- ○ _____
- ○ _____
- ○ _____
- ○ _____

OUTDOOR

- ○ _____
- ○ _____
- ○ _____
- ○ _____
- ○ _____
- ○ _____
- ○ _____

NOTES

FALL MAINTENANCE

INDOOR

○ _____
○ _____
○ _____
○ _____
○ _____
○ _____
○ _____

OUTDOOR

○ _____
○ _____
○ _____
○ _____
○ _____
○ _____
○ _____

NOTES

WINTER MAINTENANCE

INDOOR

○ _____
○ _____
○ _____
○ _____
○ _____
○ _____
○ _____

OUTDOOR

○ _____
○ _____
○ _____
○ _____
○ _____
○ _____
○ _____

NOTES

Indoor MONTHLY MAINTENANCE

JANUARY

- ◯ _____
- ◯ _____
- ◯ _____
- ◯ _____
- ◯ _____
- ◯ _____
- ◯ _____

FEBRUARY

- ◯ _____
- ◯ _____
- ◯ _____
- ◯ _____
- ◯ _____
- ◯ _____
- ◯ _____

MARCH

- ◯ _____
- ◯ _____
- ◯ _____
- ◯ _____
- ◯ _____
- ◯ _____
- ◯ _____

APRIL

- ◯ _____
- ◯ _____
- ◯ _____
- ◯ _____
- ◯ _____
- ◯ _____
- ◯ _____

MAY

- ◯ _____
- ◯ _____
- ◯ _____
- ◯ _____
- ◯ _____
- ◯ _____
- ◯ _____

JUNE

- ◯ _____
- ◯ _____
- ◯ _____
- ◯ _____
- ◯ _____
- ◯ _____
- ◯ _____

JULY

- ◯ _____
- ◯ _____
- ◯ _____
- ◯ _____
- ◯ _____
- ◯ _____
- ◯ _____

AUGUST

- ◯ _____
- ◯ _____
- ◯ _____
- ◯ _____
- ◯ _____
- ◯ _____
- ◯ _____

SEPTEMBER

- ◯ _____
- ◯ _____
- ◯ _____
- ◯ _____
- ◯ _____
- ◯ _____
- ◯ _____

OCTOBER

- ◯ _____
- ◯ _____
- ◯ _____
- ◯ _____
- ◯ _____
- ◯ _____
- ◯ _____

NOVEMBER

- ◯ _____
- ◯ _____
- ◯ _____
- ◯ _____
- ◯ _____
- ◯ _____

DECEMBER

- ◯ _____
- ◯ _____
- ◯ _____
- ◯ _____
- ◯ _____
- ◯ _____
- ◯ _____

Outdoor MONTHLY MAINTENANCE

YEAR

JANUARY
- ○ _____
- ○ _____
- ○ _____
- ○ _____
- ○ _____
- ○ _____
- ○ _____

FEBRUARY
- ○ _____
- ○ _____
- ○ _____
- ○ _____
- ○ _____
- ○ _____
- ○ _____

MARCH
- ○ _____
- ○ _____
- ○ _____
- ○ _____
- ○ _____
- ○ _____
- ○ _____

APRIL
- ○ _____
- ○ _____
- ○ _____
- ○ _____
- ○ _____
- ○ _____
- ○ _____

MAY
- ○ _____
- ○ _____
- ○ _____
- ○ _____
- ○ _____
- ○ _____
- ○ _____

JUNE
- ○ _____
- ○ _____
- ○ _____
- ○ _____
- ○ _____
- ○ _____
- ○ _____

JULY
- ○ _____
- ○ _____
- ○ _____
- ○ _____
- ○ _____
- ○ _____
- ○ _____

AUGUST
- ○ _____
- ○ _____
- ○ _____
- ○ _____
- ○ _____
- ○ _____
- ○ _____

SEPTEMBER
- ○ _____
- ○ _____
- ○ _____
- ○ _____
- ○ _____
- ○ _____
- ○ _____

OCTOBER
- ○ _____
- ○ _____
- ○ _____
- ○ _____
- ○ _____
- ○ _____

NOVEMBER
- ○ _____
- ○ _____
- ○ _____
- ○ _____
- ○ _____
- ○ _____

DECEMBER
- ○ _____
- ○ _____
- ○ _____
- ○ _____
- ○ _____
- ○ _____

WHAT TO DO DIFFERENT NEXT YEAR:

SPRING MAINTENANCE

INDOOR

- ○ _____
- ○ _____
- ○ _____
- ○ _____
- ○ _____
- ○ _____
- ○ _____

OUTDOOR

- ○ _____
- ○ _____
- ○ _____
- ○ _____
- ○ _____
- ○ _____
- ○ _____

NOTES

SUMMER MAINTENANCE

INDOOR

- ○ _____
- ○ _____
- ○ _____
- ○ _____
- ○ _____
- ○ _____
- ○ _____

OUTDOOR

- ○ _____
- ○ _____
- ○ _____
- ○ _____
- ○ _____
- ○ _____
- ○ _____

NOTES

YEAR

INDOOR

OUTDOOR

○ _____
○ _____
○ _____
○ _____
○ _____
○ _____
○ _____

○ _____
○ _____
○ _____
○ _____
○ _____
○ _____
○ _____

NOTES

WINTER MAINTENANCE

INDOOR

OUTDOOR

○ _____
○ _____
○ _____
○ _____
○ _____
○ _____
○ _____

○ _____
○ _____
○ _____
○ _____
○ _____
○ _____
○ _____

NOTES

Indoor MONTHLY MAINTENANCE

JANUARY

- ○ _____
- ○ _____
- ○ _____
- ○ _____
- ○ _____
- ○ _____
- ○ _____

FEBRUARY

- ○ _____
- ○ _____
- ○ _____
- ○ _____
- ○ _____
- ○ _____
- ○ _____

MARCH

- ○ _____
- ○ _____
- ○ _____
- ○ _____
- ○ _____
- ○ _____
- ○ _____

APRIL

- ○ _____
- ○ _____
- ○ _____
- ○ _____
- ○ _____
- ○ _____
- ○ _____

MAY

- ○ _____
- ○ _____
- ○ _____
- ○ _____
- ○ _____
- ○ _____
- ○ _____

JUNE

- ○ _____
- ○ _____
- ○ _____
- ○ _____
- ○ _____
- ○ _____
- ○ _____

JULY

- ○ _____
- ○ _____
- ○ _____
- ○ _____
- ○ _____
- ○ _____
- ○ _____

AUGUST

- ○ _____
- ○ _____
- ○ _____
- ○ _____
- ○ _____
- ○ _____
- ○ _____

SEPTEMBER

- ○ _____
- ○ _____
- ○ _____
- ○ _____
- ○ _____
- ○ _____
- ○ _____

OCTOBER

- ○ _____
- ○ _____
- ○ _____
- ○ _____
- ○ _____
- ○ _____
- ○ _____

NOVEMBER

- ○ _____
- ○ _____
- ○ _____
- ○ _____
- ○ _____
- ○ _____

DECEMBER

- ○ _____
- ○ _____
- ○ _____
- ○ _____
- ○ _____
- ○ _____

Outdoor MONTHLY MAINTENANCE

JANUARY

- ◯ _____
- ◯ _____
- ◯ _____
- ◯ _____
- ◯ _____
- ◯ _____
- ◯ _____

FEBRUARY

- ◯ _____
- ◯ _____
- ◯ _____
- ◯ _____
- ◯ _____
- ◯ _____
- ◯ _____

MARCH

- ◯ _____
- ◯ _____
- ◯ _____
- ◯ _____
- ◯ _____
- ◯ _____
- ◯ _____

APRIL

- ◯ _____
- ◯ _____
- ◯ _____
- ◯ _____
- ◯ _____
- ◯ _____
- ◯ _____

MAY

- ◯ _____
- ◯ _____
- ◯ _____
- ◯ _____
- ◯ _____
- ◯ _____
- ◯ _____

JUNE

- ◯ _____
- ◯ _____
- ◯ _____
- ◯ _____
- ◯ _____
- ◯ _____
- ◯ _____

JULY

- ◯ _____
- ◯ _____
- ◯ _____
- ◯ _____
- ◯ _____
- ◯ _____
- ◯ _____

AUGUST

- ◯ _____
- ◯ _____
- ◯ _____
- ◯ _____
- ◯ _____
- ◯ _____
- ◯ _____

SEPTEMBER

- ◯ _____
- ◯ _____
- ◯ _____
- ◯ _____
- ◯ _____
- ◯ _____
- ◯ _____

OCTOBER

- ◯ _____
- ◯ _____
- ◯ _____
- ◯ _____
- ◯ _____
- ◯ _____
- ◯ _____

NOVEMBER

- ◯ _____
- ◯ _____
- ◯ _____
- ◯ _____
- ◯ _____
- ◯ _____

DECEMBER

- ◯ _____
- ◯ _____
- ◯ _____
- ◯ _____
- ◯ _____
- ◯ _____

WHAT TO DO DIFFERENT NEXT YEAR:

SPRING MAINTENANCE

INDOOR

- ○ _____
- ○ _____
- ○ _____
- ○ _____
- ○ _____
- ○ _____
- ○ _____

OUTDOOR

- ○ _____
- ○ _____
- ○ _____
- ○ _____
- ○ _____
- ○ _____
- ○ _____

NOTES

SUMMER MAINTENANCE

INDOOR

- ○ _____
- ○ _____
- ○ _____
- ○ _____
- ○ _____
- ○ _____
- ○ _____

OUTDOOR

- ○ _____
- ○ _____
- ○ _____
- ○ _____
- ○ _____
- ○ _____
- ○ _____

NOTES

FALL MAINTENANCE

INDOOR

- ◯ _____
- ◯ _____
- ◯ _____
- ◯ _____
- ◯ _____
- ◯ _____
- ◯ _____

OUTDOOR

- ◯ _____
- ◯ _____
- ◯ _____
- ◯ _____
- ◯ _____
- ◯ _____
- ◯ _____

NOTES

WINTER MAINTENANCE

INDOOR

- ◯ _____
- ◯ _____
- ◯ _____
- ◯ _____
- ◯ _____
- ◯ _____
- ◯ _____

OUTDOOR

- ◯ _____
- ◯ _____
- ◯ _____
- ◯ _____
- ◯ _____
- ◯ _____
- ◯ _____

NOTES

Indoor MONTHLY MAINTENANCE

YEAR

JANUARY
- ◯ _____
- ◯ _____
- ◯ _____
- ◯ _____
- ◯ _____
- ◯ _____
- ◯ _____

FEBRUARY
- ◯ _____
- ◯ _____
- ◯ _____
- ◯ _____
- ◯ _____
- ◯ _____
- ◯ _____

MARCH
- ◯ _____
- ◯ _____
- ◯ _____
- ◯ _____
- ◯ _____
- ◯ _____
- ◯ _____

APRIL
- ◯ _____
- ◯ _____
- ◯ _____
- ◯ _____
- ◯ _____
- ◯ _____
- ◯ _____

MAY
- ◯ _____
- ◯ _____
- ◯ _____
- ◯ _____
- ◯ _____
- ◯ _____
- ◯ _____

JUNE
- ◯ _____
- ◯ _____
- ◯ _____
- ◯ _____
- ◯ _____
- ◯ _____
- ◯ _____

JULY
- ◯ _____
- ◯ _____
- ◯ _____
- ◯ _____
- ◯ _____
- ◯ _____
- ◯ _____

AUGUST
- ◯ _____
- ◯ _____
- ◯ _____
- ◯ _____
- ◯ _____
- ◯ _____
- ◯ _____

SEPTEMBER
- ◯ _____
- ◯ _____
- ◯ _____
- ◯ _____
- ◯ _____
- ◯ _____
- ◯ _____

OCTOBER
- ◯ _____
- ◯ _____
- ◯ _____
- ◯ _____
- ◯ _____
- ◯ _____
- ◯ _____

NOVEMBER
- ◯ _____
- ◯ _____
- ◯ _____
- ◯ _____
- ◯ _____
- ◯ _____

DECEMBER
- ◯ _____
- ◯ _____
- ◯ _____
- ◯ _____
- ◯ _____
- ◯ _____

Outdoor MONTHLY MAINTENANCE

JANUARY
- ◯ _____
- ◯ _____
- ◯ _____
- ◯ _____
- ◯ _____
- ◯ _____
- ◯ _____

FEBRUARY
- ◯ _____
- ◯ _____
- ◯ _____
- ◯ _____
- ◯ _____
- ◯ _____
- ◯ _____

MARCH
- ◯ _____
- ◯ _____
- ◯ _____
- ◯ _____
- ◯ _____
- ◯ _____
- ◯ _____

APRIL
- ◯ _____
- ◯ _____
- ◯ _____
- ◯ _____
- ◯ _____
- ◯ _____
- ◯ _____

MAY
- ◯ _____
- ◯ _____
- ◯ _____
- ◯ _____
- ◯ _____
- ◯ _____
- ◯ _____

JUNE
- ◯ _____
- ◯ _____
- ◯ _____
- ◯ _____
- ◯ _____
- ◯ _____
- ◯ _____

JULY
- ◯ _____
- ◯ _____
- ◯ _____
- ◯ _____
- ◯ _____
- ◯ _____
- ◯ _____

AUGUST
- ◯ _____
- ◯ _____
- ◯ _____
- ◯ _____
- ◯ _____
- ◯ _____
- ◯ _____

SEPTEMBER
- ◯ _____
- ◯ _____
- ◯ _____
- ◯ _____
- ◯ _____
- ◯ _____
- ◯ _____

OCTOBER
- ◯ _____
- ◯ _____
- ◯ _____
- ◯ _____
- ◯ _____
- ◯ _____
- ◯ _____

NOVEMBER
- ◯ _____
- ◯ _____
- ◯ _____
- ◯ _____
- ◯ _____
- ◯ _____

DECEMBER
- ◯ _____
- ◯ _____
- ◯ _____
- ◯ _____
- ◯ _____
- ◯ _____

WHAT TO DO DIFFERENT NEXT YEAR:

SPRING MAINTENANCE

INDOOR

○ _____
○ _____
○ _____
○ _____
○ _____
○ _____
○ _____

OUTDOOR

○ _____
○ _____
○ _____
○ _____
○ _____
○ _____
○ _____

NOTES

SUMMER MAINTENANCE

INDOOR

○ _____
○ _____
○ _____
○ _____
○ _____
○ _____
○ _____

OUTDOOR

○ _____
○ _____
○ _____
○ _____
○ _____
○ _____
○ _____

NOTES

YEAR

FALL MAINTENANCE

INDOOR

- ○ _____
- ○ _____
- ○ _____
- ○ _____
- ○ _____
- ○ _____
- ○ _____

OUTDOOR

- ○ _____
- ○ _____
- ○ _____
- ○ _____
- ○ _____
- ○ _____
- ○ _____

NOTES

WINTER MAINTENANCE

INDOOR

- ○ _____
- ○ _____
- ○ _____
- ○ _____
- ○ _____
- ○ _____
- ○ _____

OUTDOOR

- ○ _____
- ○ _____
- ○ _____
- ○ _____
- ○ _____
- ○ _____
- ○ _____

NOTES

Indoor **MONTHLY MAINTENANCE**

JANUARY

- ◯ _____
- ◯ _____
- ◯ _____
- ◯ _____
- ◯ _____
- ◯ _____
- ◯ _____

FEBRUARY

- ◯ _____
- ◯ _____
- ◯ _____
- ◯ _____
- ◯ _____
- ◯ _____
- ◯ _____

MARCH

- ◯ _____
- ◯ _____
- ◯ _____
- ◯ _____
- ◯ _____
- ◯ _____
- ◯ _____

APRIL

- ◯ _____
- ◯ _____
- ◯ _____
- ◯ _____
- ◯ _____
- ◯ _____
- ◯ _____

MAY

- ◯ _____
- ◯ _____
- ◯ _____
- ◯ _____
- ◯ _____
- ◯ _____
- ◯ _____

JUNE

- ◯ _____
- ◯ _____
- ◯ _____
- ◯ _____
- ◯ _____
- ◯ _____
- ◯ _____

JULY

- ◯ _____
- ◯ _____
- ◯ _____
- ◯ _____
- ◯ _____
- ◯ _____
- ◯ _____

AUGUST

- ◯ _____
- ◯ _____
- ◯ _____
- ◯ _____
- ◯ _____
- ◯ _____
- ◯ _____

SEPTEMBER

- ◯ _____
- ◯ _____
- ◯ _____
- ◯ _____
- ◯ _____
- ◯ _____
- ◯ _____

OCTOBER

- ◯ _____
- ◯ _____
- ◯ _____
- ◯ _____
- ◯ _____
- ◯ _____
- ◯ _____

NOVEMBER

- ◯ _____
- ◯ _____
- ◯ _____
- ◯ _____
- ◯ _____
- ◯ _____
- ◯ _____

DECEMBER

- ◯ _____
- ◯ _____
- ◯ _____
- ◯ _____
- ◯ _____
- ◯ _____
- ◯ _____

Outdoor MONTHLY MAINTENANCE

YEAR

JANUARY

○ _____
○ _____
○ _____
○ _____
○ _____
○ _____
○ _____

FEBRUARY

○ _____
○ _____
○ _____
○ _____
○ _____
○ _____
○ _____

MARCH

○ _____
○ _____
○ _____
○ _____
○ _____
○ _____
○ _____

APRIL

○ _____
○ _____
○ _____
○ _____
○ _____
○ _____
○ _____

MAY

○ _____
○ _____
○ _____
○ _____
○ _____
○ _____
○ _____

JUNE

○ _____
○ _____
○ _____
○ _____
○ _____
○ _____
○ _____

JULY

○ _____
○ _____
○ _____
○ _____
○ _____
○ _____
○ _____

AUGUST

○ _____
○ _____
○ _____
○ _____
○ _____
○ _____
○ _____

SEPTEMBER

○ _____
○ _____
○ _____
○ _____
○ _____
○ _____
○ _____

OCTOBER

○ _____
○ _____
○ _____
○ _____
○ _____
○ _____
○ _____

NOVEMBER

○ _____
○ _____
○ _____
○ _____
○ _____
○ _____
○ _____

DECEMBER

○ _____
○ _____
○ _____
○ _____
○ _____
○ _____
○ _____

WHAT TO DO DIFFERENT NEXT YEAR:

SPRING MAINTENANCE

INDOOR

- ◯ _____
- ◯ _____
- ◯ _____
- ◯ _____
- ◯ _____
- ◯ _____
- ◯ _____

OUTDOOR

- ◯ _____
- ◯ _____
- ◯ _____
- ◯ _____
- ◯ _____
- ◯ _____
- ◯ _____

NOTES

SUMMER MAINTENANCE

INDOOR

- ◯ _____
- ◯ _____
- ◯ _____
- ◯ _____
- ◯ _____
- ◯ _____
- ◯ _____

OUTDOOR

- ◯ _____
- ◯ _____
- ◯ _____
- ◯ _____
- ◯ _____
- ◯ _____
- ◯ _____

NOTES

YEAR

FALL MAINTENANCE

INDOOR

- ○ _____
- ○ _____
- ○ _____
- ○ _____
- ○ _____
- ○ _____
- ○ _____

OUTDOOR

- ○ _____
- ○ _____
- ○ _____
- ○ _____
- ○ _____
- ○ _____
- ○ _____

NOTES

WINTER MAINTENANCE

INDOOR

- ○ _____
- ○ _____
- ○ _____
- ○ _____
- ○ _____
- ○ _____
- ○ _____

OUTDOOR

- ○ _____
- ○ _____
- ○ _____
- ○ _____
- ○ _____
- ○ _____
- ○ _____

NOTES

Indoor MONTHLY MAINTENANCE

JANUARY
- ◯ _____
- ◯ _____
- ◯ _____
- ◯ _____
- ◯ _____
- ◯ _____
- ◯ _____

FEBRUARY
- ◯ _____
- ◯ _____
- ◯ _____
- ◯ _____
- ◯ _____
- ◯ _____
- ◯ _____

MARCH
- ◯ _____
- ◯ _____
- ◯ _____
- ◯ _____
- ◯ _____
- ◯ _____
- ◯ _____

APRIL
- ◯ _____
- ◯ _____
- ◯ _____
- ◯ _____
- ◯ _____
- ◯ _____
- ◯ _____

MAY
- ◯ _____
- ◯ _____
- ◯ _____
- ◯ _____
- ◯ _____
- ◯ _____
- ◯ _____

JUNE
- ◯ _____
- ◯ _____
- ◯ _____
- ◯ _____
- ◯ _____
- ◯ _____
- ◯ _____

JULY
- ◯ _____
- ◯ _____
- ◯ _____
- ◯ _____
- ◯ _____
- ◯ _____
- ◯ _____

AUGUST
- ◯ _____
- ◯ _____
- ◯ _____
- ◯ _____
- ◯ _____
- ◯ _____
- ◯ _____

SEPTEMBER
- ◯ _____
- ◯ _____
- ◯ _____
- ◯ _____
- ◯ _____
- ◯ _____
- ◯ _____

OCTOBER
- ◯ _____
- ◯ _____
- ◯ _____
- ◯ _____
- ◯ _____
- ◯ _____
- ◯ _____

NOVEMBER
- ◯ _____
- ◯ _____
- ◯ _____
- ◯ _____
- ◯ _____
- ◯ _____
- ◯ _____

DECEMBER
- ◯ _____
- ◯ _____
- ◯ _____
- ◯ _____
- ◯ _____
- ◯ _____
- ◯ _____

Outdoor MONTHLY MAINTENANCE

JANUARY
- ⭕ _____
- ⭕ _____
- ⭕ _____
- ⭕ _____
- ⭕ _____
- ⭕ _____
- ⭕ _____

FEBRUARY
- ⭕ _____
- ⭕ _____
- ⭕ _____
- ⭕ _____
- ⭕ _____
- ⭕ _____
- ⭕ _____

MARCH
- ⭕ _____
- ⭕ _____
- ⭕ _____
- ⭕ _____
- ⭕ _____
- ⭕ _____
- ⭕ _____

APRIL
- ⭕ _____
- ⭕ _____
- ⭕ _____
- ⭕ _____
- ⭕ _____
- ⭕ _____
- ⭕ _____

MAY
- ⭕ _____
- ⭕ _____
- ⭕ _____
- ⭕ _____
- ⭕ _____
- ⭕ _____
- ⭕ _____

JUNE
- ⭕ _____
- ⭕ _____
- ⭕ _____
- ⭕ _____
- ⭕ _____
- ⭕ _____
- ⭕ _____

JULY
- ⭕ _____
- ⭕ _____
- ⭕ _____
- ⭕ _____
- ⭕ _____
- ⭕ _____
- ⭕ _____

AUGUST
- ⭕ _____
- ⭕ _____
- ⭕ _____
- ⭕ _____
- ⭕ _____
- ⭕ _____
- ⭕ _____

SEPTEMBER
- ⭕ _____
- ⭕ _____
- ⭕ _____
- ⭕ _____
- ⭕ _____
- ⭕ _____
- ⭕ _____

OCTOBER
- ⭕ _____
- ⭕ _____
- ⭕ _____
- ⭕ _____
- ⭕ _____
- ⭕ _____
- ⭕ _____

NOVEMBER
- ⭕ _____
- ⭕ _____
- ⭕ _____
- ⭕ _____
- ⭕ _____
- ⭕ _____
- ⭕ _____

DECEMBER
- ⭕ _____
- ⭕ _____
- ⭕ _____
- ⭕ _____
- ⭕ _____
- ⭕ _____
- ⭕ _____

WHAT TO DO DIFFERENT NEXT YEAR:

SPRING MAINTENANCE

INDOOR

- ○ _____
- ○ _____
- ○ _____
- ○ _____
- ○ _____
- ○ _____
- ○ _____

OUTDOOR

- ○ _____
- ○ _____
- ○ _____
- ○ _____
- ○ _____
- ○ _____
- ○ _____

NOTES

SUMMER MAINTENANCE

INDOOR

- ○ _____
- ○ _____
- ○ _____
- ○ _____
- ○ _____
- ○ _____
- ○ _____

OUTDOOR

- ○ _____
- ○ _____
- ○ _____
- ○ _____
- ○ _____
- ○ _____
- ○ _____

NOTES

YEAR

INDOOR

- ◯ _____
- ◯ _____
- ◯ _____
- ◯ _____
- ◯ _____
- ◯ _____
- ◯ _____

OUTDOOR

- ◯ _____
- ◯ _____
- ◯ _____
- ◯ _____
- ◯ _____
- ◯ _____
- ◯ _____

NOTES

WINTER MAINTENANCE

INDOOR

- ◯ _____
- ◯ _____
- ◯ _____
- ◯ _____
- ◯ _____
- ◯ _____
- ◯ _____

OUTDOOR

- ◯ _____
- ◯ _____
- ◯ _____
- ◯ _____
- ◯ _____
- ◯ _____
- ◯ _____

NOTES

Indoor MONTHLY MAINTENANCE

JANUARY

- ◯ _____
- ◯ _____
- ◯ _____
- ◯ _____
- ◯ _____
- ◯ _____
- ◯ _____

FEBRUARY

- ◯ _____
- ◯ _____
- ◯ _____
- ◯ _____
- ◯ _____
- ◯ _____
- ◯ _____

MARCH

- ◯ _____
- ◯ _____
- ◯ _____
- ◯ _____
- ◯ _____
- ◯ _____
- ◯ _____

APRIL

- ◯ _____
- ◯ _____
- ◯ _____
- ◯ _____
- ◯ _____
- ◯ _____
- ◯ _____

MAY

- ◯ _____
- ◯ _____
- ◯ _____
- ◯ _____
- ◯ _____
- ◯ _____
- ◯ _____

JUNE

- ◯ _____
- ◯ _____
- ◯ _____
- ◯ _____
- ◯ _____
- ◯ _____
- ◯ _____

JULY

- ◯ _____
- ◯ _____
- ◯ _____
- ◯ _____
- ◯ _____
- ◯ _____
- ◯ _____

AUGUST

- ◯ _____
- ◯ _____
- ◯ _____
- ◯ _____
- ◯ _____
- ◯ _____
- ◯ _____

SEPTEMBER

- ◯ _____
- ◯ _____
- ◯ _____
- ◯ _____
- ◯ _____
- ◯ _____
- ◯ _____

OCTOBER

- ◯ _____
- ◯ _____
- ◯ _____
- ◯ _____
- ◯ _____
- ◯ _____
- ◯ _____

NOVEMBER

- ◯ _____
- ◯ _____
- ◯ _____
- ◯ _____
- ◯ _____
- ◯ _____

DECEMBER

- ◯ _____
- ◯ _____
- ◯ _____
- ◯ _____
- ◯ _____
- ◯ _____
- ◯ _____

Outdoor MONTHLY MAINTENANCE

YEAR

JANUARY

- ○
- ○
- ○
- ○
- ○
- ○
- ○

FEBRUARY

- ○
- ○
- ○
- ○
- ○
- ○
- ○

MARCH

- ○
- ○
- ○
- ○
- ○
- ○
- ○

APRIL

- ○
- ○
- ○
- ○
- ○
- ○
- ○

MAY

- ○
- ○
- ○
- ○
- ○
- ○
- ○

JUNE

- ○
- ○
- ○
- ○
- ○
- ○
- ○

JULY

- ○
- ○
- ○
- ○
- ○
- ○
- ○

AUGUST

- ○
- ○
- ○
- ○
- ○
- ○
- ○

SEPTEMBER

- ○
- ○
- ○
- ○
- ○
- ○
- ○

OCTOBER

- ○
- ○
- ○
- ○
- ○
- ○
- ○

NOVEMBER

- ○
- ○
- ○
- ○
- ○
- ○

DECEMBER

- ○
- ○
- ○
- ○
- ○
- ○

WHAT TO DO DIFFERENT NEXT YEAR:

SPRING MAINTENANCE

INDOOR

- ○ _____
- ○ _____
- ○ _____
- ○ _____
- ○ _____
- ○ _____
- ○ _____

OUTDOOR

- ○ _____
- ○ _____
- ○ _____
- ○ _____
- ○ _____
- ○ _____
- ○ _____

NOTES

SUMMER MAINTENANCE

INDOOR

- ○ _____
- ○ _____
- ○ _____
- ○ _____
- ○ _____
- ○ _____
- ○ _____

OUTDOOR

- ○ _____
- ○ _____
- ○ _____
- ○ _____
- ○ _____
- ○ _____
- ○ _____

NOTES

FALL MAINTENANCE

INDOOR

○ _____
○ _____
○ _____
○ _____
○ _____
○ _____
○ _____

OUTDOOR

○ _____
○ _____
○ _____
○ _____
○ _____
○ _____
○ _____

NOTES

WINTER MAINTENANCE

INDOOR

○ _____
○ _____
○ _____
○ _____
○ _____
○ _____
○ _____

OUTDOOR

○ _____
○ _____
○ _____
○ _____
○ _____
○ _____
○ _____

NOTES

Indoor **MONTHLY MAINTENANCE**

JANUARY
- ◯ _____
- ◯ _____
- ◯ _____
- ◯ _____
- ◯ _____
- ◯ _____
- ◯ _____

FEBRUARY
- ◯ _____
- ◯ _____
- ◯ _____
- ◯ _____
- ◯ _____
- ◯ _____
- ◯ _____

MARCH
- ◯ _____
- ◯ _____
- ◯ _____
- ◯ _____
- ◯ _____
- ◯ _____
- ◯ _____

APRIL
- ◯ _____
- ◯ _____
- ◯ _____
- ◯ _____
- ◯ _____
- ◯ _____
- ◯ _____

MAY
- ◯ _____
- ◯ _____
- ◯ _____
- ◯ _____
- ◯ _____
- ◯ _____
- ◯ _____

JUNE
- ◯ _____
- ◯ _____
- ◯ _____
- ◯ _____
- ◯ _____
- ◯ _____
- ◯ _____

JULY
- ◯ _____
- ◯ _____
- ◯ _____
- ◯ _____
- ◯ _____
- ◯ _____
- ◯ _____

AUGUST
- ◯ _____
- ◯ _____
- ◯ _____
- ◯ _____
- ◯ _____
- ◯ _____
- ◯ _____

SEPTEMBER
- ◯ _____
- ◯ _____
- ◯ _____
- ◯ _____
- ◯ _____
- ◯ _____
- ◯ _____

OCTOBER
- ◯ _____
- ◯ _____
- ◯ _____
- ◯ _____
- ◯ _____
- ◯ _____
- ◯ _____

NOVEMBER
- ◯ _____
- ◯ _____
- ◯ _____
- ◯ _____
- ◯ _____
- ◯ _____
- ◯ _____

DECEMBER
- ◯ _____
- ◯ _____
- ◯ _____
- ◯ _____
- ◯ _____
- ◯ _____
- ◯ _____

Outdoor MONTHLY MAINTENANCE

JANUARY

- ◯ _____
- ◯ _____
- ◯ _____
- ◯ _____
- ◯ _____
- ◯ _____
- ◯ _____

FEBRUARY

- ◯ _____
- ◯ _____
- ◯ _____
- ◯ _____
- ◯ _____
- ◯ _____
- ◯ _____

MARCH

- ◯ _____
- ◯ _____
- ◯ _____
- ◯ _____
- ◯ _____
- ◯ _____
- ◯ _____

APRIL

- ◯ _____
- ◯ _____
- ◯ _____
- ◯ _____
- ◯ _____
- ◯ _____
- ◯ _____

MAY

- ◯ _____
- ◯ _____
- ◯ _____
- ◯ _____
- ◯ _____
- ◯ _____
- ◯ _____

JUNE

- ◯ _____
- ◯ _____
- ◯ _____
- ◯ _____
- ◯ _____
- ◯ _____
- ◯ _____

JULY

- ◯ _____
- ◯ _____
- ◯ _____
- ◯ _____
- ◯ _____
- ◯ _____
- ◯ _____

AUGUST

- ◯ _____
- ◯ _____
- ◯ _____
- ◯ _____
- ◯ _____
- ◯ _____
- ◯ _____

SEPTEMBER

- ◯ _____
- ◯ _____
- ◯ _____
- ◯ _____
- ◯ _____
- ◯ _____
- ◯ _____

OCTOBER

- ◯ _____
- ◯ _____
- ◯ _____
- ◯ _____
- ◯ _____
- ◯ _____

NOVEMBER

- ◯ _____
- ◯ _____
- ◯ _____
- ◯ _____
- ◯ _____
- ◯ _____

DECEMBER

- ◯ _____
- ◯ _____
- ◯ _____
- ◯ _____
- ◯ _____
- ◯ _____

WHAT TO DO DIFFERENT NEXT YEAR:

SPRING MAINTENANCE

INDOOR

- ○ _____
- ○ _____
- ○ _____
- ○ _____
- ○ _____
- ○ _____
- ○ _____

OUTDOOR

- ○ _____
- ○ _____
- ○ _____
- ○ _____
- ○ _____
- ○ _____
- ○ _____

NOTES

SUMMER MAINTENANCE

INDOOR

- ○ _____
- ○ _____
- ○ _____
- ○ _____
- ○ _____
- ○ _____
- ○ _____

OUTDOOR

- ○ _____
- ○ _____
- ○ _____
- ○ _____
- ○ _____
- ○ _____
- ○ _____

NOTES

YEAR

FALL MAINTENANCE

INDOOR

- ○ _____
- ○ _____
- ○ _____
- ○ _____
- ○ _____
- ○ _____
- ○ _____

OUTDOOR

- ○ _____
- ○ _____
- ○ _____
- ○ _____
- ○ _____
- ○ _____
- ○ _____

NOTES

WINTER MAINTENANCE

INDOOR

- ○ _____
- ○ _____
- ○ _____
- ○ _____
- ○ _____
- ○ _____
- ○ _____

OUTDOOR

- ○ _____
- ○ _____
- ○ _____
- ○ _____
- ○ _____
- ○ _____
- ○ _____

NOTES

Indoor **MONTHLY MAINTENANCE**

JANUARY

- ◯ _____
- ◯ _____
- ◯ _____
- ◯ _____
- ◯ _____
- ◯ _____
- ◯ _____

FEBRUARY

- ◯ _____
- ◯ _____
- ◯ _____
- ◯ _____
- ◯ _____
- ◯ _____
- ◯ _____

MARCH

- ◯ _____
- ◯ _____
- ◯ _____
- ◯ _____
- ◯ _____
- ◯ _____
- ◯ _____

APRIL

- ◯ _____
- ◯ _____
- ◯ _____
- ◯ _____
- ◯ _____
- ◯ _____
- ◯ _____

MAY

- ◯ _____
- ◯ _____
- ◯ _____
- ◯ _____
- ◯ _____
- ◯ _____
- ◯ _____

JUNE

- ◯ _____
- ◯ _____
- ◯ _____
- ◯ _____
- ◯ _____
- ◯ _____
- ◯ _____

JULY

- ◯ _____
- ◯ _____
- ◯ _____
- ◯ _____
- ◯ _____
- ◯ _____
- ◯ _____

AUGUST

- ◯ _____
- ◯ _____
- ◯ _____
- ◯ _____
- ◯ _____
- ◯ _____
- ◯ _____

SEPTEMBER

- ◯ _____
- ◯ _____
- ◯ _____
- ◯ _____
- ◯ _____
- ◯ _____
- ◯ _____

OCTOBER

- ◯ _____
- ◯ _____
- ◯ _____
- ◯ _____
- ◯ _____
- ◯ _____
- ◯ _____

NOVEMBER

- ◯ _____
- ◯ _____
- ◯ _____
- ◯ _____
- ◯ _____
- ◯ _____
- ◯ _____

DECEMBER

- ◯ _____
- ◯ _____
- ◯ _____
- ◯ _____
- ◯ _____
- ◯ _____
- ◯ _____

Outdoor MONTHLY MAINTENANCE

JANUARY

- ○ _____
- ○ _____
- ○ _____
- ○ _____
- ○ _____
- ○ _____
- ○ _____

FEBRUARY

- ○ _____
- ○ _____
- ○ _____
- ○ _____
- ○ _____
- ○ _____
- ○ _____

MARCH

- ○ _____
- ○ _____
- ○ _____
- ○ _____
- ○ _____
- ○ _____
- ○ _____

APRIL

- ○ _____
- ○ _____
- ○ _____
- ○ _____
- ○ _____
- ○ _____
- ○ _____

MAY

- ○ _____
- ○ _____
- ○ _____
- ○ _____
- ○ _____
- ○ _____
- ○ _____

JUNE

- ○ _____
- ○ _____
- ○ _____
- ○ _____
- ○ _____
- ○ _____
- ○ _____

JULY

- ○ _____
- ○ _____
- ○ _____
- ○ _____
- ○ _____
- ○ _____
- ○ _____

AUGUST

- ○ _____
- ○ _____
- ○ _____
- ○ _____
- ○ _____
- ○ _____
- ○ _____

SEPTEMBER

- ○ _____
- ○ _____
- ○ _____
- ○ _____
- ○ _____
- ○ _____
- ○ _____

OCTOBER

- ○ _____
- ○ _____
- ○ _____
- ○ _____
- ○ _____
- ○ _____
- ○ _____

NOVEMBER

- ○ _____
- ○ _____
- ○ _____
- ○ _____
- ○ _____
- ○ _____

DECEMBER

- ○ _____
- ○ _____
- ○ _____
- ○ _____
- ○ _____
- ○ _____

WHAT TO DO DIFFERENT NEXT YEAR:

SAFETY INSPECTIONS *Log*

SMOKE DETECTOR		CARBON MONOXIDE DETECTOR		FIRE EXTINGUISHER	
REPLACE BATTERIES DATE	CHECK FUNCTION DATE	REPLACE BATTERIES DATE	CHECK FUNCTION DATE	CHECK PRESSURE GAUGE DATE	INSPECT FOR DEFECTS DATE

SAFETY INSPECTIONS log

SMOKE DETECTOR	
REPLACE BATTERIES DATE	CHECK FUNCTION DATE

CARBON MONOXIDE DETECTOR	
REPLACE BATTERIES DATE	CHECK FUNCTION DATE

FIRE EXTINGUISHER	
CHECK PRESSURE GAUGE DATE	INSPECT FOR DEFECTS DATE

ANNUAL HOME SECURITY SYSTEM

EXTERIOR LIGHTS MONTHLY CHECK

YEAR _____   YEAR _____

YEAR _____   YEAR _____

YEAR _____   YEAR _____

PERIMETER CHECKS WEEKLY   YEAR _____

JAN					JULY					
FEB					AUG					
MAR					SEPT					
APR					OCT					
MAY					NOV					
JUNE					DEC					

PERIMETER CHECKS WEEKLY   YEAR _____

JAN					JULY					
FEB					AUG					
MAR					SEPT					
APR					OCT					
MAY					NOV					
JUNE					DEC					

PERIMETER CHECKS WEEKLY   YEAR _____

JAN					JULY					
FEB					AUG					
MAR					SEPT					
APR					OCT					
MAY					NOV					
JUNE					DEC					

INSPECTION *log*

PERIMETER CHECKS WEEKLY
YEAR _____

JAN					JULY					
FEB					AUG					
MAR					SEPT					
APR					OCT					
MAY					NOV					
JUNE					DEC					

PERIMETER CHECKS WEEKLY
YEAR _____

JAN					JULY					
FEB					AUG					
MAR					SEPT					
APR					OCT					
MAY					NOV					
JUNE					DEC					

PERIMETER CHECKS WEEKLY
YEAR _____

JAN					JULY					
FEB					AUG					
MAR					SEPT					
APR					OCT					
MAY					NOV					
JUNE					DEC					

CONTROL PANEL QUARTERLY CHECKS

YEAR _____   YEAR _____

YEAR _____   YEAR _____

YEAR _____   YEAR _____

ANNUAL INSPECTION BY A PROFESSIONAL

CHECK CAMERAS DAILY

ANNUAL HOME SECURITY SYSTEM

EXTERIOR LIGHTS MONTHLY CHECK

YEAR _____   YEAR _____

YEAR _____   YEAR _____

YEAR _____   YEAR _____

PERIMETER CHECKS WEEKLY

YEAR _____

JAN					JULY				
FEB					AUG				
MAR					SEPT				
APR					OCT				
MAY					NOV				
JUNE					DEC				

PERIMETER CHECKS WEEKLY

YEAR _____

JAN					JULY				
FEB					AUG				
MAR					SEPT				
APR					OCT				
MAY					NOV				
JUNE					DEC				

PERIMETER CHECKS WEEKLY

YEAR _____

JAN					JULY				
FEB					AUG				
MAR					SEPT				
APR					OCT				
MAY					NOV				
JUNE					DEC				

INSPECTION *log*

PERIMETER CHECKS WEEKLY

YEAR _____

JAN					JULY				
FEB					AUG				
MAR					SEPT				
APR					OCT				
MAY					NOV				
JUNE					DEC				

PERIMETER CHECKS WEEKLY

YEAR _____

JAN					JULY				
FEB					AUG				
MAR					SEPT				
APR					OCT				
MAY					NOV				
JUNE					DEC				

PERIMETER CHECKS WEEKLY

YEAR _____

JAN					JULY				
FEB					AUG				
MAR					SEPT				
APR					OCT				
MAY					NOV				
JUNE					DEC				

CONTROL PANEL QUARTERLY CHECKS

YEAR _____	YEAR _____

YEAR _____	YEAR _____

YEAR _____	YEAR _____

ANNUAL INSPECTION BY A PROFESSIONAL

CHECK CAMERAS DAILY

HVAC FILTERS *Log*

FURNACE		AIR CLEANER		HUMIDIFIER	
SIZE:		SIZE:		SIZE:	
DATE:		DATE:		DATE:	
DATE:		DATE:		DATE:	
DATE:		DATE:		DATE:	
DATE:		DATE:		DATE:	
DATE:		DATE:		DATE:	
DATE:		DATE:		DATE:	
DATE:		DATE:		DATE:	
DATE:		DATE:		DATE:	
DATE:		DATE:		DATE:	
DATE:		DATE:		DATE:	
DATE:		DATE:		DATE:	
DATE:		DATE:		DATE:	
DATE:		DATE:		DATE:	
DATE:		DATE:		DATE:	
DATE:		DATE:		DATE:	
DATE:		DATE:		DATE:	
DATE:		DATE:		DATE:	
DATE:		DATE:		DATE:	
DATE:		DATE:		DATE:	
DATE:		DATE:		DATE:	
DATE:		DATE:		DATE:	
DATE:		DATE:		DATE:	
DATE:		DATE:		DATE:	

HVAC FILTERS *Log*

FURNACE	
SIZE:	
DATE:	
DATE:	
DATE:	
DATE:	
DATE:	
DATE:	
DATE:	
DATE:	
DATE:	
DATE:	
DATE:	
DATE:	
DATE:	
DATE:	
DATE:	
DATE:	
DATE:	
DATE:	
DATE:	
DATE:	
DATE:	
DATE:	

AIR CLEANER	
SIZE:	
DATE:	
DATE:	
DATE:	
DATE:	
DATE:	
DATE:	
DATE:	
DATE:	
DATE:	
DATE:	
DATE:	
DATE:	
DATE:	
DATE:	
DATE:	
DATE:	
DATE:	
DATE:	
DATE:	
DATE:	
DATE:	
DATE:	

HUMIDIFIER	
SIZE:	
DATE:	
DATE:	
DATE:	
DATE:	
DATE:	
DATE:	
DATE:	
DATE:	
DATE:	
DATE:	
DATE:	
DATE:	
DATE:	
DATE:	
DATE:	
DATE:	
DATE:	
DATE:	
DATE:	
DATE:	
DATE:	
DATE:	

PEST CONTROL

COMPANY NAME	APPLICATION DATE	APPLICATION TYPE	NEXT DUE DATE

PEST CONTROL *Log*

COMPANY NAME	APPLICATION DATE	APPLICATION TYPE	NEXT DUE DATE

HOME IMPROVEMENT *Wishlist*

PRIORITY	ROOM	DESIRED IMPROVEMENT
☆☆☆☆		
☆☆☆☆		
☆☆☆☆		
☆☆☆☆		
☆☆☆☆		
☆☆☆☆		
☆☆☆☆		
☆☆☆☆		
☆☆☆☆		
☆☆☆☆		
☆☆☆☆		
☆☆☆☆		
☆☆☆☆		
☆☆☆☆		

NOTES

SKETCH AREA

HOME IMPROVEMENT *Wishlist*

PRIORITY	ROOM	DESIRED IMPROVEMENT
☆☆☆☆		
☆☆☆☆		
☆☆☆☆		
☆☆☆☆		
☆☆☆☆		
☆☆☆☆		
☆☆☆☆		
☆☆☆☆		
☆☆☆☆		
☆☆☆☆		
☆☆☆☆		
☆☆☆☆		
☆☆☆☆		
☆☆☆☆		

NOTES

SKETCH AREA

HOME UPGRADE *Log*

ITEM	ROOM	DATE	MANUFACTURER/VENDER
Windows			
Siding			
Cabinets			
Carpet			
Roof			
HVAC			
Room Additions			
Landscape			
Hardscape			

NOTES

NOTES

HOME UPGRADE *Log*

ITEM	ROOM	DATE	MANUFACTURER/VENDER
Windows			
Siding			
Cabinets			
Carpet			
Roof			
HVAC			
Room Additions			
Landscape			
Hardscape			

NOTES

NOTES

PAINTING *log*

ROOM		DATE PAINTED	PAINT BRAND	COLOR #	FINISH Ex. Eggshell, flat, satin, etc.	LEFTOVER PAINT LOCTAION
	WALLS					
	TRIM					
	WALLS					
	TRIM					
	WALLS					
	TRIM					
	WALLS					
	TRIM					
	WALLS					
	TRIM					
	WALLS					
	TRIM					
	WALLS					
	TRIM					
	WALLS					
	TRIM					
	WALLS					
	TRIM					
	WALLS					
	TRIM					

PAINTING *Log*

ROOM		DATE PAINTED	PAINT BRAND	COLOR #	FINISH Ex. Eggshell, flat, satin, etc.	LEFTOVER PAINT LOCTAION
	WALLS					
	TRIM					
	WALLS					
	TRIM					
	WALLS					
	TRIM					
	WALLS					
	TRIM					
	WALLS					
	TRIM					
	WALLS					
	TRIM					
	WALLS					
	TRIM					
	WALLS					
	TRIM					
	WALLS					
	TRIM					
	WALLS					
	TRIM					

PAINTING *Log*

ROOM		DATE PAINTED	PAINT BRAND	COLOR #	FINISH Ex. Eggshell, flat, satin, etc.	LEFTOVER PAINT LOCTAION
	WALLS					
	TRIM					
	WALLS					
	TRIM					
	WALLS					
	TRIM					
	WALLS					
	TRIM					
	WALLS					
	TRIM					
	WALLS					
	TRIM					
	WALLS					
	TRIM					
	WALLS					
	TRIM					
	WALLS					
	TRIM					
	WALLS					
	TRIM					

PAINTING

ROOM		DATE PAINTED	PAINT BRAND	COLOR #	FINISH Ex. Eggshell, flat, satin, etc.	LEFTOVER PAINT LOCTAION
	WALLS					
	TRIM					
	WALLS					
	TRIM					
	WALLS					
	TRIM					
	WALLS					
	TRIM					
	WALLS					
	TRIM					
	WALLS					
	TRIM					
	WALLS					
	TRIM					
	WALLS					
	TRIM					
	WALLS					
	TRIM					
	WALLS					
	TRIM					

FOYER *log*

AT MOVE-IN

	Manufacturer	Model/Serial #	Warranty Terms
Lighting			
Flooring			

REPLACEMENT

Item	Date	Manufacturer	Model/Serial #	Warranty Terms

SKETCH AREA

LIVING ROOM *Log*

AT MOVE-IN

	Manufacturer	Model/Serial #	Warranty Terms
Fireplace			
Ceiling Fan			
Flooring			
Lighting			

REPLACEMENT

Item	Date	Manufacturer	Model/Serial #	Warranty Terms

SKETCH AREA

FAMILY/GREAT ROOM *Log*

AT MOVE-IN

	Manufacturer	Model/Serial #	Warranty Terms
Fireplace			
Ceiling Fan			
Flooring			
Lighting			
Cabinets/Built-ins			

REPLACEMENT

Item	Date	Manufacturer	Model/Serial #	Warranty Terms

SKETCH AREA

DINING ROOM *Log*

AT MOVE-IN

	Manufacturer	Model/Serial #	Warranty Terms
Fireplace			
Ceiling Fan			
Flooring			
Lighting			

REPLACEMENT

Item	Date	Manufacturer	Model/Serial #	Warranty Terms

SKETCH AREA

BONUS ROOM *Log*

AT MOVE-IN

	Manufacturer	Model/Serial #	Warranty Terms
Flooring			
Lighting			
Cabinets/Built-ins			

REPLACEMENT

Item	Date	Manufacturer	Model/Serial #	Warranty Terms

SKETCH AREA

KITCHEN Log

AT MOVE-IN

	Manufacturer	Model/Serial #	Warranty Terms
Refrigerator			
Stove			
Microwave			
Garbage Disposal			
Dishwasher			
Wine Cooler			
Flooring			
Cabinets			

REPLACEMENT

Item	Date	Manufacturer	Model/Serial #	Warranty Terms

SKETCH AREA

MUD ROOM *log*

AT MOVE-IN

	Manufacturer	Model/Serial #	Warranty Terms
Cabinets/Built-ins			
Lighting			
Flooring			

REPLACEMENT

Item	Date	Manufacturer	Model/Serial #	Warranty Terms

SKETCH AREA

LAUNDRY ROOM *Log*

AT MOVE-IN

	Manufacturer	Model/Serial #	Warranty Terms
Washer			
Dryer			
Cabinets			

REPLACEMENT

Item	Date	Manufacturer	Model/Serial #	Warranty Terms

SKETCH AREA

MASTER BEDROOM/ON-SUITE *Log*

AT MOVE-IN

	Manufacturer	Model/Serial #	Warranty Terms
Flooring			
Ceiling Fan			
Vanity			
Toilet			
Tub/Shower			
Tile			

REPLACEMENT

Item	Date	Manufacturer	Model/Serial #	Warranty Terms

SKETCH AREA

MASTER CLOSET *log*

AT MOVE-IN

	Description
Flooring	
Shelving	
Built-Ins	
Lighting	

REPLACEMENT

Item	Date	Manufacturer	Model/Serial #	Warranty Terms

SKETCH AREA

OTHER CLOSETS *Log*

AT MOVE-IN

	Description
Bedroom - 1	
Bedroom - 2	
Bedroom - 3	
Bedroom - 4	
Coat Closet	

REPLACEMENT

Item	Date	Manufacturer	Model/Serial #	Warranty Terms

SKETCH AREA

BEDROOMS *Log*

	Manufacturer	Model/Serial #	Warranty Terms
Flooring - 1			
Ceiling Fan - 1			
Flooring - 2			
Ceiling Fan - 2			

REPLACEMENT

Item	Date	Manufacturer	Model/Serial #	Warranty Terms

SKETCH AREA

BEDROOMS *log*

AT MOVE-IN

	Manufacturer	Model/Serial #	Warranty Terms
Flooring - 3			
Ceiling Fan - 3			
Flooring - 4			
Ceiling Fan - 4			

REPLACEMENT

Item	Date	Manufacturer	Model/Serial #	Warranty Terms

SKETCH AREA

_____ BATHROOM _Log_

AT MOVE-IN

	Manufacturer	Model/Serial #	Warranty Terms
Flooring			
Cabinets			
Shower			
Tub			
Toilet			
Wall Tile			

REPLACEMENT

Item	Date	Manufacturer	Model/Serial #	Warranty Terms

SKETCH AREA

BATHROOM *Log*

AT MOVE-IN

	Manufacturer	Model/Serial #	Warranty Terms
Flooring			
Cabinets			
Shower			
Tub			
Toilet			
Wall Tile			

REPLACEMENT

Item	Date	Manufacturer	Model/Serial #	Warranty Terms

SKETCH AREA

_____ BATHROOM *Log*

AT MOVE-IN

	Manufacturer	Model/Serial #	Warranty Terms
Flooring			
Cabinets			
Shower			
Tub			
Toilet			
Wall Tile			

REPLACEMENT

Item	Date	Manufacturer	Model/Serial #	Warranty Terms

SKETCH AREA

ROOM *Log*

AT MOVE-IN

	Manufacturer	Model/Serial #	Warranty Terms
Flooring			
Ceiling Fan			
Cabinets/Built-ins			

REPLACEMENT

Item	Date	Manufacturer	Model/Serial #	Warranty Terms

SKETCH AREA

ROOM *log*

AT MOVE-IN

	Manufacturer	Model/Serial #	Warranty Terms
Flooring			
Ceiling Fan			
Cabinets/Built-ins			

REPLACEMENT

Item	Date	Manufacturer	Model/Serial #	Warranty Terms

SKETCH AREA

UTILITY ROOM *log*

AT MOVE-IN

	Manufacturer	Model/Serial #	Warranty Terms
Hot Water Heater			
Water Softener			
Furnace			
Humidifier			
Air Conditioner			
Sump Pump			

REPLACEMENT

Item	Date	Manufacturer	Model/Serial #	Warranty Terms

SKETCH AREA

BASEMENT *log*

AT MOVE-IN

	Manufacturer	Model/Serial #	Warranty Terms
Ceiling			
Flooring			
Cabinets/Built-ins			

REPLACEMENT

Item	Date	Manufacturer	Model/Serial #	Warranty Terms

SKETCH AREA

GARAGE *log*

AT MOVE-IN

	Manufacturer	Model/Serial #	Warranty Terms
Flooring			
Garage Door			
Garage Door Opener			
Storage			

REPLACEMENT

Item	Date	Manufacturer	Model/Serial #	Warranty Terms

SKETCH AREA

EXTERIOR

	Manufacturer	Model/Serial #	Warranty Terms
Windows			
Siding			
Painted Areas			
Gutters/Down Spouts			
Roof			

REPLACEMENT

Item	Date	Manufacturer	Model/Serial #	Warranty Terms

SKETCH AREA

Room INVENTORY
for insurance purposes

LIVINGROOM

FURNITURE	ELECTRONICS	APPLIANCES	VALUABLES

NOTES

FAMILY ¦ GREAT ROOM

FURNITURE	ELECTRONICS	APPLIANCES	VALUABLES

NOTES

Room INVENTORY
for insurance purposes

OFFICE

FURNITURE	ELECTRONICS	APPLIANCES	VALUABLES

NOTES

LOFT AREA

FURNITURE	ELECTRONICS	APPLIANCES	VALUABLES

NOTES

Room INVENTORY
for insurance purposes

DINING ROOM

FURNITURE	ELECTRONICS	APPLIANCES	VALUABLES

NOTES

FOYER

FURNITURE	ELECTRONICS	APPLIANCES	VALUABLES

NOTES

Room INVENTORY
for insurance purposes

KITCHEN

FURNITURE	ELECTRONICS	APPLIANCES	VALUABLES

NOTES

MUD ROOM

FURNITURE	ELECTRONICS	APPLIANCES	VALUABLES

NOTES

Room INVENTORY
for insurance purposes

LAUNDRY

FURNITURE	ELECTRONICS	APPLIANCES	VALUABLES

NOTES

MASTER SUITE

FURNITURE	ELECTRONICS	APPLIANCES	VALUABLES

NOTES

Room INVENTORY
for insurance purposes

BEDROOM 1

FURNITURE	ELECTRONICS	APPLIANCES	VALUABLES

NOTES

BEDROOM 2

FURNITURE	ELECTRONICS	APPLIANCES	VALUABLES

NOTES

Room INVENTORY
for insurance purposes

BEDROOM 3

FURNITURE	ELECTRONICS	APPLIANCES	VALUABLES

NOTES

BEDROOM 4

FURNITURE	ELECTRONICS	APPLIANCES	VALUABLES

NOTES

Room INVENTORY
for insurance purposes

BATHROOM FURNITURE	ELECTRONICS	APPLIANCES	VALUABLES

NOTES

BATHROOM FURNITURE	ELECTRONICS	APPLIANCES	VALUABLES

NOTES

Room INVENTORY
for insurance purposes

BATHROOM

FURNITURE	ELECTRONICS	APPLIANCES	VALUABLES

NOTES

ATTIC

FURNITURE	ELECTRONICS	APPLIANCES	VALUABLES

NOTES

Room INVENTORY
for insurance purposes

UTILITY ROOM

FURNITURE	ELECTRONICS	APPLIANCES	VALUABLES

NOTES

BASEMENT

FURNITURE	ELECTRONICS	APPLIANCES	VALUABLES

NOTES

Room INVENTORY
for insurance purposes

GARAGE

FURNITURE	ELECTRONICS	APPLIANCES	VALUABLES

NOTES

OUT BUILDINGS

FURNITURE	ELECTRONICS	APPLIANCES	VALUABLES

NOTES

Room INVENTORY
for insurance purposes

FURNITURE	ELECTRONICS	APPLIANCES	VALUABLES

NOTES

FURNITURE	ELECTRONICS	APPLIANCES	VALUABLES

NOTES

Room INVENTORY
for insurance purposes

FURNITURE	ELECTRONICS	APPLIANCES	VALUABLES

NOTES

FURNITURE	ELECTRONICS	APPLIANCES	VALUABLES

NOTES

NOTES

DIY PROJECT *log*

PROJECT NAME:		START DATE:	
BUDGET:		FINISH DATE:	
PRIORITY:	☆ ☆ ☆ ☆ ☆	FINAL COST:	

ACTION STEPS	MATERIALS NEEDED

SKETCH AREA

DIY PROJECT *log*

PROJECT NAME:		START DATE:	
BUDGET:		FINISH DATE:	
PRIORITY:	☆ ☆ ☆ ☆ ☆	FINAL COST:	

ACTION STEPS	MATERIALS NEEDED

SKETCH AREA

DIY PROJECT *log*

PROJECT NAME:		START DATE:	
BUDGET:		FINISH DATE:	
PRIORITY:	☆ ☆ ☆ ☆ ☆	FINAL COST:	

ACTION STEPS	MATERIALS NEEDED

SKETCH AREA

DIY PROJECT *Log*

PROJECT NAME:		START DATE:	
BUDGET:		FINISH DATE:	
PRIORITY:	☆ ☆ ☆ ☆ ☆	FINAL COST:	

ACTION STEPS	MATERIALS NEEDED

SKETCH AREA

DIY PROJECT *log*

PROJECT NAME:		START DATE:	
BUDGET:		FINISH DATE:	
PRIORITY:	☆ ☆ ☆ ☆ ☆	FINAL COST:	

ACTION STEPS	MATERIALS NEEDED

SKETCH AREA

DIY PROJECT *log*

PROJECT NAME:		START DATE:	
BUDGET:		FINISH DATE:	
PRIORITY:	☆ ☆ ☆ ☆ ☆	FINAL COST:	

ACTION STEPS	MATERIALS NEEDED

SKETCH AREA

DIY PROJECT *log*

PROJECT NAME:		START DATE:	
BUDGET:		FINISH DATE:	
PRIORITY:	☆ ☆ ☆ ☆ ☆	FINAL COST:	

ACTION STEPS	MATERIALS NEEDED

SKETCH AREA

DIY PROJECT *Log*

PROJECT NAME:		START DATE:	
BUDGET:		FINISH DATE:	
PRIORITY:	☆ ☆ ☆ ☆ ☆	FINAL COST:	

ACTION STEPS	MATERIALS NEEDED

SKETCH AREA

DIY PROJECT *log*

PROJECT NAME:		START DATE:	
BUDGET:		FINISH DATE:	
PRIORITY:	☆ ☆ ☆ ☆ ☆	FINAL COST:	

ACTION STEPS

MATERIALS NEEDED

SKETCH AREA

DIY PROJECT *Log*

PROJECT NAME:		START DATE:	
BUDGET:		FINISH DATE:	
PRIORITY:	☆ ☆ ☆ ☆ ☆	FINAL COST:	

ACTION STEPS

MATERIALS NEEDED

SKETCH AREA

NOTES

Made in the USA
Coppell, TX
12 October 2024

38557104R00103